THE SOWER
LESSONS ON CHRISTIAN GROWTH

THE NAMES OF CHRIST ILLUSTRATRED

ACTIVITY BOOK

THE NOC ILLUSTRATED ACTIVITY BOOKS: AN AMAZING WAY TO TEACH YOUTH THE MANY DIFFERENT CHARACTERS OF CHRIST FOUND IN THE HOLY SCRIPTURES.

ISBN: 1-441-46172-8

PRINTED IN THE UNITED STATES OF AMERICA

COVER PAGE DESIGNED BY DYNAMIC ANIMATION PRODUCTIONS, LLC

PREFACE

"AND HE SPAKE MANY THINGS UNTO THEM IN PARABLES, SAYING, BEHOLD, A SOWER WENT FORTH TO SOW." MATTHEW 13:3 (KJV)

TO OUR PARENTS, TEACHERS AND GUARDIANS: IT IS A PRIVILEGE TO STUDY GOD'S WORD WITH YOUR CHILDREN AND A BLESSING TO TRAIN AND DISCIPLINE THEM FOR SERVICE IN THE MASTER'S CAUSE. ALONG WITH THEIR BIBLES, WE STRONGLY ENCOURAGE YOUR PARTICIPATION IN THE CHILD'S USAGE OF THIS ACTIVITY BOOK.

GROWTH SPURTS

UNSCRAMBLE THE MISSING LETTERS TO FIGURE OUT THE PHRASE BELOW

GENESIS 16:10

AND THE ANGEL OF THE LORD SAID UNT__ HER, I WILL MULTIPLY THY SEED EXCEEDINGLY, THAT IT SHALL NOT BE NUMBERE__ FOR MULTITUDE.

GENESIS 1:11

AND GOD SAID, LET THE EARTH BRING FORTH __RASS, THE HERB YIELD-ING __EED, AND THE FRUIT TREE YIELDING FRUIT AFTER HIS KIND, WHOSE SEED IS IN ITSELF, UPON THE EARTH: AND IT WAS SO.

ISAIAH 45:25

IN TH__ LORD SHALL ALL THE SEED OF __SRAEL BE JUSTIFIED, AND SHALL GLORY.

LEVITICUS 26:5

AND YOUR THRESHING SHALL R__ACH UNTO THE VINTAGE, AND THE VIN-TAGE SHALL REACH UNTO THE SO__ING TIME: AND YE SHALL EAT YOUR BREAD TO THE FULL, AND DWELL IN YOUR LAND SAFELY.

LEVITICUS 11:37

AND IF ANY PART OF THEIR CARCASE FALL UPO__ ANY SOWING SEED WHICH IS TO BE SOWN, IT SHALL BE CLEAN.

THE SECRET PHRASE IS:

S __ __ __   __ __ __ __ __ __

SECRET PHRASE 1: ANSWERS FOUND ON PAGE 35

FILL IN THE BLANK
COMMIT THESE VERSES OF SCRIPTURE TO MEMORY

NOW LEARN A _____ OF THE _____ TREE; WHEN HER _____ IS YET _____, AND PUTTETH FORTH _____, YE KNOW THAT _____ IS NEAR. ~ MARK 13:28

NOW THE _____ IS THIS: THE _____ IS THE _____ OF GOD. ~ LUKE 8:11

IT IS LIKE A _____ OF _____ SEED, WHICH A MAN _____, AND _____ INTO HIS _____; AND IT _____, AND _____ A GREAT _____; AND THE _____ OF THE AIR _____ IN THE _____ OF IT. ~ LUKE 13:19

THERE WAS A CERTAIN _____ WHICH HAD TWO _____: THE ONE OWED FIVE _____ PENCE, AND THE OTHER _____. ~ LUKE 7:41

AND HE WENT AND _____ HIMSELF TO A _____ OF THAT _____; AND HE SENT HIM INTO HIS _____ TO FEED _____. ~ LUKE 15:15

AND BY _____ THERE CAME DOWN A CERTAIN _____ THAT _____: AND WHEN HE _____ HIM, HE _____ BY ON THE _____ SIDE. ~ LUKE 10:31

THEY THAT WERE _____ TOOK THEIR _____, AND TOOK NO _____ WITH _____. ~ MATTHEW 25:3

BUT THE _____ SAID TO HIS _____, BRING _____ THE BEST _____, AND _____ IT ON _____; AND PUT A _____ ON HIS _____, AND _____ ON HIS _____. ~ LUKE 15:22

TWO _____ WENT UP INTO THE _____ TO _____; THE ONE A _____, AND THE OTHER A _____. ~ LUKE 18:10

KEYS TO CHRISTIAN GROWTH

Crossword Puzzle 1

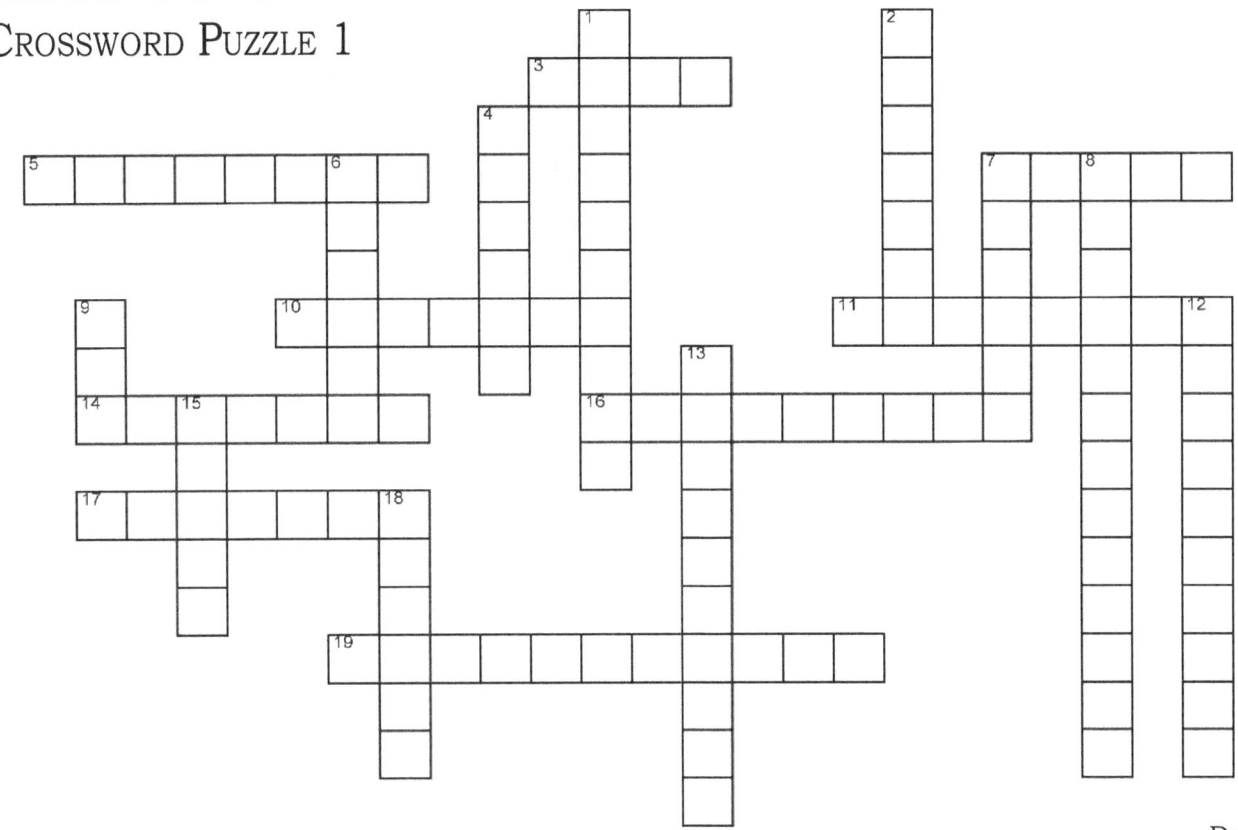

Across

3. That from which any thing grows; first principle; original.

5. Freedom from pride and arrogance. A deep sense of one's own unworthiness in the sight of God.

7. To apply the mind to. The pursuit of knowledge, as by reading, observation, or research.

10. The act or process of gathering a crop. The product of labor.

11. Softness of temper; mildness; gentleness; self-control under injuries and provocations.

14. To bear testimony; to give evidence. To attest; to testify to something.

16. Compliance with a command. Dutiful or submissive behavior with respect to another.

17. Receiving as the fruit of labor or the reward of works.

19. The act of putting something to a special use or purpose.

Down

1. A quality, endowment or acquirement completely excellent or of great worth. Without error.

2. Use, purpose; that which is required by God of man.

4. A solemn address to the supreme being, confession of our sins, supplication for mercy and forgiveness, and thanksgiving, or an expression of gratitude to God for His mercies and benefits.

6. Experience; suffering that puts strength, patience of faith to the test.

7. An implement having a semicircular blade attached to a short handle, used for cutting grain or tall grass.

8. To know thoroughly by close contact or long experience with. Comprehending.

9. To scatter seed over the ground for growing. To impregnate a growing medium with seed.

12. Sacrifice of one's own desires or interests.

13. That which is presented to the mind as an inducement to evil.

15. To instruct; to communicate knowledge to another.

18. The history of the birth, life, actions, death, resurrection, ascension and doctrines of Jesus Christ.

Crossword Puzzle 1: Answers found on page 37

SECRET MESSAGE 1

A	B	C	D	E	F	G	H	I	J	K	L	M	N	O	P	Q	R	S	T	U	V	W	X	Y	Z
9	4	15	21	26	10	18	5	16	1	13	6	23	8	2	14	24	11	3	17	25	7	19	12	20	22

USE THE ABOVE KEYS TO DECODE THE MESSAGE BELOW

17 5 2 25   3 5 9 6 17   8 2 17

3 2 19   17 5 20   7 16 8 26 20 9 11 21

19 16 17 5   21 16 7 26 11 3   3 26 26 21 3 :

6 26 3 17   17 5 26   10 11 25 16 17   2 10

17 5 20   3 26 26 21   19 5 16 15 5

17 5 2 25   5 9 3 17   3 2 19 8 ,   9 8 21

17 5 26   10 11 25 16 17   2 10   17 5 20

7 16 8 26 20 9 11 21 ,   4 26

21 26 10 16 6 26 21 .

WHERE IS THIS TEXT FOUND: _____

SEE HOW MANY WORDS
YOU CAN GROW OUT OF
GARDEN TOOLS

"AND THE LORD GOD PLANTED A GARDEN EASTWARD IN EDEN; AND THERE HE PUT THE MAN WHOM HE HAD FORMED." ~ GENESIS 2:8

BIBLE TRIVIA 1: LESSONS FROM THE PARABLES

1. IN THE PARABLE OF THE GOOD SAMARITAN, WHO WAS THE FIRST PERSON TO PASS BY THE WOUNDED MAN?
A) PHARISEE   B) SAMARITAN   C) PRIEST   D) SCRIBE

2. IN THE PARABLE OF THE DEBTORS, ONE OWED 500 PENCE. HOW MUCH DID THE OTHER ONE OWE?
A) 5   B) 50   C) 100   D) 5000

3. WHEN THE PRODIGAL SON RETURNED, HIS FATHER GAVE HIM A ROBE, SHOES AND WHAT OTHER ITEM?
A) RING   B) COIN   C) PEARL   D) FISH

4. WHICH ONE OF THE FOLLOWING WAS THE KINGDOM NOT LIKENED TO?
A) LEAVEN   B) FISHING NET   C) HIDDEN TREASURE   D) VINEYARD

5. TWO MEN WENT UP TO THE TEMPLE TO PRAY, A PHARISEE AND WHO ELSE?
A) PUBLICAN   B) SCRIBE   C) JEW   D) GENTILE

6. IN THE PARABLE OF THE FIG TREE, WHAT IS NEAR WHEN YOU SEE THIS TREE PUTTING FORTH LEAVES?
A) SPRING   B) SUMMER   C) AUTUMN   D) WINTER

7. FIVE OF THE "TEN VIRGINS" DID NOT TAKE ENOUGH OF WHAT?
A) FOOD   B) CLOTHING   C) OIL   D) WATER

8. IN THE PARABLE OF THE SOWER, WHAT DOES THE SEED REPRESENT?
A) BELIEVERS   B) JESUS   C) GENTILES   D) WORD OF GOD

9. IN THE PARABLE OF THE MUSTARD SEED, WHAT DO THE BIRDS COME AND DO WHEN IT BECOMES A TREE?
A) LODGE IN THEM   B) EAT THE LEAVES   C) REST FOR THE NIGHT   D) DIE

10. AFTER THE PRODIGAL SON SPENT ALL HIS MONEY AND FAMINE HAD COME, WHAT JOB DID HE GET?
A) BUILDING HOUSES   B) FEEDING PIGS   C) SWEEPING STREETS   D) HERDING SHEEP

BIBLE TRIVIA 1: ANSWERS FOUND ON PAGE 34

COLORING ACTIVITY

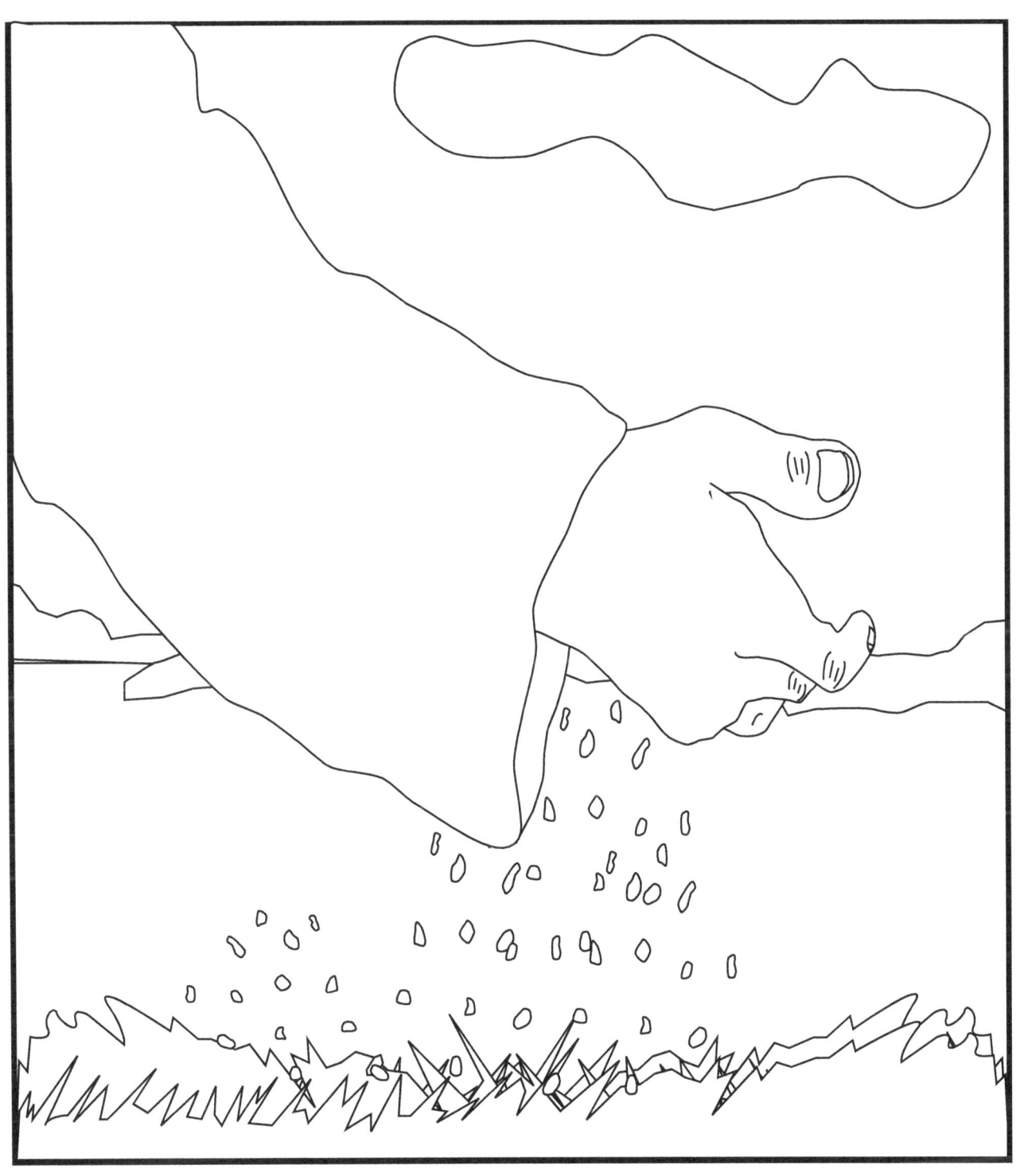

THE SOWER

GROWTH SPURTS

UNSCRAMBLE THE MISSING LETTERS TO FIGURE OUT THE PHRASE BELOW

MATTHEW 9:38

PRAY Y__ THEREFORE THE LORD OF THE HARVEST, THAT HE WILL SEND FORTH LABOU__ERS INTO HIS HARVEST.

JOEL 3:13

PUT YE IN THE SICKLE, FOR __HE HARVEST IS RIPE: COME, GET YOU DOWN; FOR THE PRESS IS FULL, THE FATS OVERFLOW; FOR __HEIR WICKEDNESS IS __REAT.

JEREMIAH 8:20

THE HARVEST IS PAST, THE SU__MER IS ENDED, AND WE __RE NOT SAVED.

ISAIAH 9:3

THOU HAST MULTIPLIED THE __ATION, AND NOT INCREASED THE JOY: THEY JOY BEFORE T__EE ACCORDING TO THE JOY IN HARVEST, AND A__ MEN REJOICE WHEN THEY DIV_DE THE SPOIL.

RUTH 2:23

SO SHE KEPT FAST BY THE MAIDENS OF BOAZ TO GL__AN UNTO THE END OF BARLEY HARVEST AND OF WHEAT HAR__EST; AND DWELT WITH HER MOTHER _N LAW.

THE SECRET PHRASE IS:

__ __ __ __ __ __ __ __ __ __ __   __ __ __ __

SECRET PHRASE 2: ANSWER FOUND ON PAGE 35

UNSCRAMBLE THESE WORDS THAT PROMOTE GROWTH

EHRTVSA

_____

INSWETS

_____

CFIPNROTEE

_____

VEIESCR

_____

WOMDIS

_____

EGRCA

_____

FACTNOTSICANII

_____

PNIAIPLTCOA

_____

SAILTR

_____

HYCITRA

_____

UNSCRAMBLIE EXERCISE 1: ANSWERS FOUND ON PAGE 34

THINGS TO CULTIVATE
CROSSWORD PUZZLE 2

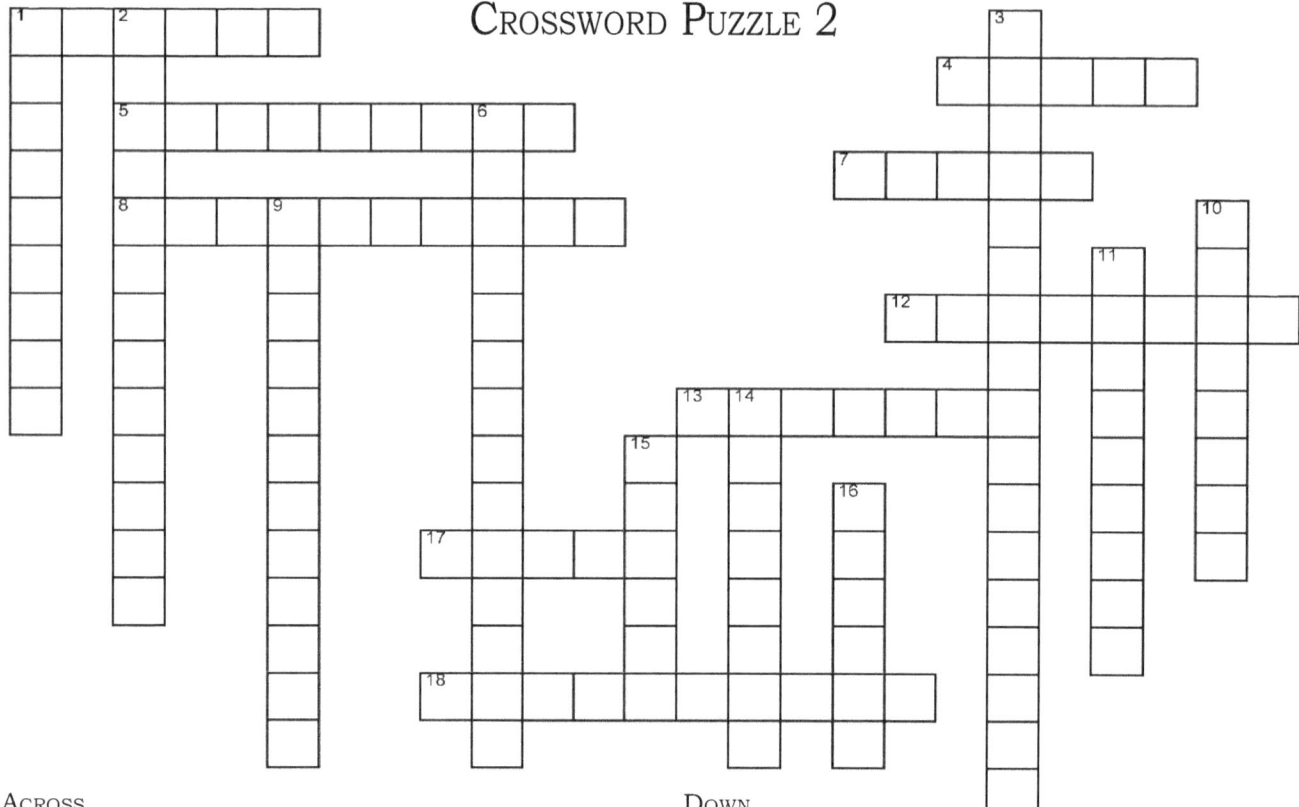

ACROSS

1. THE ANOINTED; A TITLE GIVEN TO THE SAVIOR OF THE WORLD. MESSIAH.

4. THE STATE OF BEING PROTECTED OR SANCTIFIED BY THE FAVOR OF GOD.

5. A RELIGIOUS LIFE; A CAREFUL OBSERVANCE OF THE LAWS OF GOD AND PERFORMANCE OF RELIGIOUS DUTIES, PROCEEDING FROM LOVE AND REVERENCE FOR THE DIVINE CHARACTER AND COMMANDS; CHRISTIAN OBEDIENCE.

7. CONFIDENT BELIEF IN THE TRUTH, VALUE, OR TRUSTWORTHINESS OF A PERSON, IDEA, OR THING.

8. MODERATION AND SELF-RESTRAINT, AS IN BEHAVIOR OR EXPRESSION. PATIENCE; CALMNESS; SEDATENESS.

12. FIRMNESS; SOLIDITY OR TOUGHNESS. THE ABILITY TO MAINTAIN A MORAL OR INTELLECTUAL POSITION FIRMLY.

13. THAT DISPOSITION OF HEART WHICH INCLINES MEN TO THINK FAVORABLY OF THEIR FELLOW MEN AND TO DO THEM GOOD. SOMETHING GIVEN TO HELP THE NEEDY.

17. A GRACIOUS, FRIENDLY, OR OBLIGING ACT THAT IS FREELY GRANTED; KIND REGARD; KINDNESS.

18. A CHANGE OF HEART, OR DISPOSITIONS, IN WHICH THE ENMITY OF THE HEART TO GOD AND HIS LAW AND THE OBSTINACY OF THE WILL ARE SUBDUED, AND ARE SUCCEEDED BY SUPREME LOVE TO GOD AND HIS MORAL GOVERNMENT, AND A REFORMATION OF LIFE.

DOWN

1. A BODY OF CHRISTIANS WITH A COMMON RELIGIOUS FAITH WHO PRACTICE THE SAME DOCTRINE AND DISCIPLINE.

2. CONFORMITY OF HEART AND LIFE TO THE DIVINE LAW. MORALLY UPRIGHT.

3. KIND; AFFECTIONATE TOWARD OUR FELLOWMAN.

6. TO SET APART FOR SACRED USE; CONSECRATE.

9. A CLEANSING FROM GUILT OR THE POLLUTION OF SIN; THE EXTINCTION OF SINFUL DESIRES, APPETITES AND INCLINATIONS. CLEANSING OR PURIFYING.

10. ENDURANCE WITHOUT MURMURING OR FRETFULNESS. SELF-CONTROL WITHOUT COMPLAINT.

11. THE SUM OR RANGE OF WHAT HAS BEEN PERCEIVED, DISCOVERED, OR LEARNED. LEARNING.

14. APPLIED TO HUMAN BEINGS, HOLINESS IS PURITY OF HEART OR DISPOSITIONS; SANCTIFIED AFFECTIONS; PIETY; MORAL GOODNESS, BUT NOT PERFECT.

15. STRENGTH, BRAVERY, MORAL GOODNESS OR A VOLUNTARY OBEDIENCE TO TRUTH. MORAL EXCELLENCE AND RIGHTEOUSNESS.

16. THE ABILITY TO DISCERN OR JUDGE WHAT IS TRUE, RIGHT, OR LASTING; INSIGHT. COMMON SENSE; GOOD JUDGMENT.

CROSSWORD PUZZLE 2: ANSWERS FOUND ON PAGE 37

SEE HOW MANY WORDS
YOU CAN GROW OUT OF

ORGANIC

"It is sown a natural body; it is raised a spiritual body. There is a natural body, and there is a spiritual body." ~ 1 Corinthians 15:44

_____

_____

_____

_____   _____

_____   _____

_____   _____

_____   _____

KEYS TO GARDENING

FIND THESE WORDS IN THE FOREST OF LETTERS

```
R K I L V T G X P R A Y E R S O W Y U S Z U T A A
P K S L B G R B L K V W I T N E S S N U F N H W A
S P K E I V O I E J N F B F Y F N W D C U B E W A
P E S I R W W C A A H M F Q B O T N E M N Y K Q Z
I G O K J V N I R L W Y T Z I J J I R O J W U Y K
P U A Z D E I A A Y S F Q T A P D Q S D Y G M Z U
L M Y T I P H C T K W F A V R E Q G T N S O G Q N
C O K D H C E I E J Y C S K E V C G A C E S P L W
U U E L A N L R S D I Y T S A S D N N B L P X O J
U B P E K I T G F L F C U G P T M P D S F E M B D
O L T X M K C I P E A B D T I D M O I P D L A E A
H J D U R V S P K D C X X S N W W L N M E F W B Z
R D H H V D A N A W J T A B G D X P G X N M V D U
Y H A R V E S T V D I J I H I J I A E N I R I E Q
Q I U E D T E M P T A T I O N F I U I C A G R R L
Z K R F D V Y S B V G W K A N N P O M G L C S H X
Y S I C K L E W M E E K N E S S G D V M U K V T J
```

SEED	SOW	SICKLE
HARVEST	PERFECTION	TEMPTATION
TRIALS	PRAYER	STUDY
WITNESS	SERVICE	GOSPEL
TEACH	APPLICATION	UNDERSTANDING
REAPING	SELF DENIAL	MEEKNESS
HUMILITY	OBEDIENCE	

WORD SEARCH 1: ANSWERS FOUND ON PAGE 36

SECRET MESSAGE 2

A	B	C	D	E	F	G	H	I	J	K	L	M	N	O	P	Q	R	S	T	U	V	W	X	Y	Z
22	16	10	4	1	8	13	20	25	14	2	12	19	26	11	3	15	21	24	9	5	23	7	17	6	18

USE THE ABOVE KEYS TO DECODE THE MESSAGE BELOW

22 26 4   24 11 7   9 20 1

8 25 1 12 4 24 ,   22 26 4

3 12 22 26 9   23 25 26 1 6 22 21 4 24 ,

7 20 25 10 20   19 22 6   6 25 1 12 4

8 21 5 25 9 24   11 8   25 26 10 21 1 22 24 1 .

WHERE IS THIS TEXT FOUND? _____

"GROWTH IS ESSENTIAL IN THE WORD OF GOD"
SEEK AND FIND YOUR WAY THROUGH THE MAZE BELOW

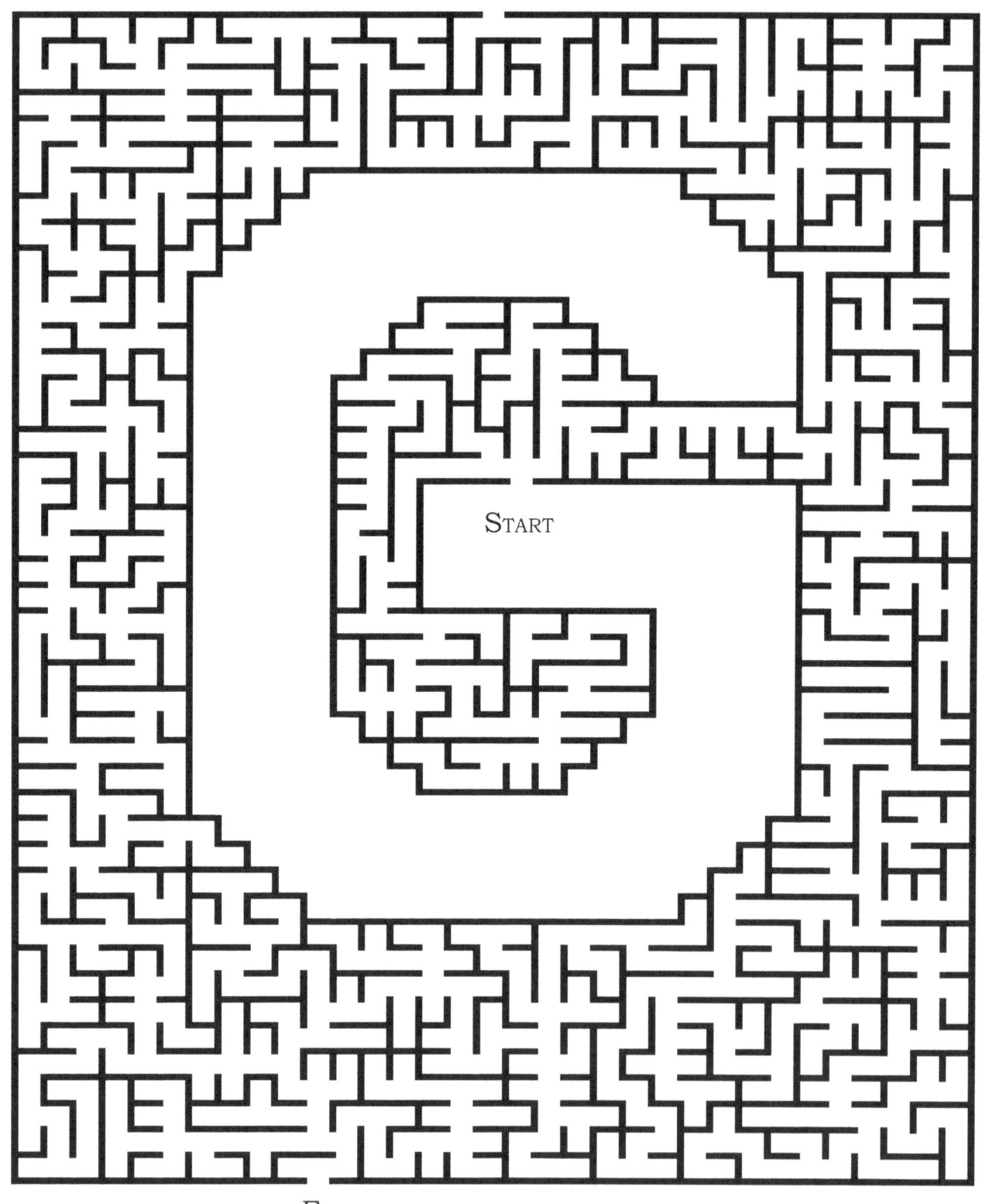

START

END

SEE HOW MANY WORDS
YOU CAN GROW OUT OF

HARVEST

"BUT NOW BEING MADE FREE FROM SIN, AND BECOME SERVANTS TO GOD, YE HAVE YOUR FRUIT UNTO HOLINESS, AND THE END EVERLASTING LIFE." ~ ROMANS 6:22

CULTIVATION

FIND THESE WORDS IN THE FOREST OF LETTERS

```
S Y R I G H T E O U S N E S S I B F A I T H J R H
F K N B R O T H E R L Y K I N D N E S S Q C Q K M
Y X Q H Y I C F W E Z Y K D R O F H T K V U A N W
B I T V T V C H D W O J P A H I N S O M F I S O I
U L Y T S E X T A L O S D U V P A T I E N C E W S
W K I D B B M R X R U T G M R L D D J O L E S L D
N F W I F J Q P J W I B H O L I N E S S F F G E O
M J K N X P N R E Z C T I U D H F V X U F F R D M
V K I P I R H T P R Y L Y O T L B I W T Z I A G S
K S A N C T I F I C A T I O N L I L C C B I C E C
E C O S Y B S X D M P N H D U J S N V A H P E C F
P K Y L F A V O R H Z F C K C B I S E I T R L Z S
D R Q F R E Z U B X E U K E S X D C W S R I I C X
C N C O N V E R S I O N S O H L T A P Z S T O S F
R K D X F V B C O M M U N I O N A Z U H N D U N T
T I H Z P T N L X P F D V U A X Y S N Z I J C E T
Y Q F Y D T A Z O B W X S T R E N G T H F D L A F
```

CONVERSION	FAITH	VIRTUE
FAVOR	KNOWLEDGE	TEMPERANCE
STRENGTH	PATIENCE	GODLINESS
HOLINESS	CHARITY	RIGHTEOUSNESS
GRACE	BROTHERLY KINDNESS	CHRIST
WISDOM	SANCTIFICATION	PURIFICATION
COMMUNION		

WORD SEARCH 2: ANSWERS FOUND ON PAGE 36

FILL IN THE BLANK
COMMIT THESE VERSES OF SCRIPTURE TO MEMORY

AND OUT OF THE _____ MADE THE LORD GOD TO _____ EVERY _____ THAT IS _____ TO THE _____, AND _____ FOR _____; THE _____ OF _____ ALSO IN THE _____ OF THE _____, AND THE TREE OF _____ OF _____ AND _____. ~ GENESIS 2:9

AND THE LORD GOD _____ A GARDEN _____ IN _____; AND THERE HE _____ THE _____ WHOM HE HAD _____. ~ GENESIS 2:8

THEREFORE THEY SHALL _____ AND _____ IN THE _____ OF ZION, AND SHALL _____ TOGETHER TO THE _____ OF THE LORD, FOR _____, AND FOR _____, AND FOR _____, AND FOR THE _____ OF THE _____ AND OF THE _____: AND THEIR _____ SHALL BE AS A _____ GARDEN; AND THEY SHALL NOT _____ ANY MORE AT ALL. ~ JEREMIAH 31:12

SOW TO _____ IN _____, _____ IN _____; _____ UP YOUR _____ GROUND: FOR IT IS _____ TO _____ THE LORD, TILL HE _____ AND RAIN _____ UPON YOU. ~ HOSEA 10:12

AND _____ THIS, _____ ALL _____, _____ TO YOUR FAITH _____; AND TO VIRTUE _____; AND TO KNOWLEDGE _____; AND TO TEMPER-ANCE _____; AND TO PATIENCE _____; AND TO GODLINESS _____ _____; AND TO BROTHERLY KINDNESS _____. ~ 2 PETER 1:5-7

OR _____ HE IT _____ FOR OUR _____? FOR OUR SAKES, NO _____, THIS IS _____: THAT HE THAT _____ SHOULD _____ IN _____; AND THAT HE THAT _____ IN _____ SHOULD BE _____ OF HIS _____. ~ 1 CORINTHIANS 9:10

ABC's of GARDENING
Crossword Puzzle 3

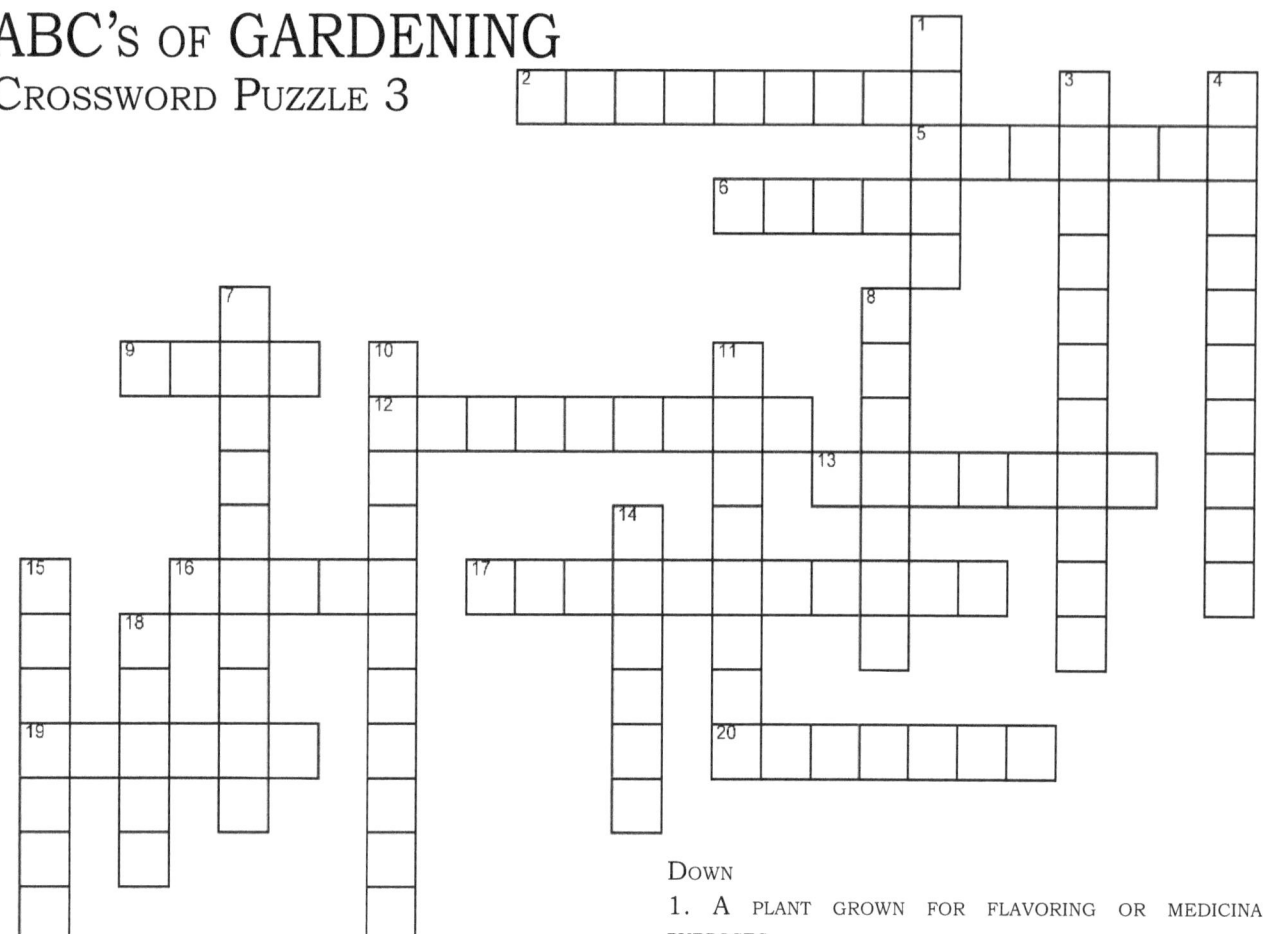

Across

2. A PLANT ADAPTED TO LIVING IN A DRY ARID HABITAT; A DESERT PLANT.

5. A CIRCULAR CLUSTER OF LEAVES THAT RADIATE FROM A CENTER AT OR CLOSE TO THE GROUND, AS IN THE DANDELION.

6. A WOODY PLANT OF RELATIVELY LOW HEIGHT, HAVING SEVERAL STEMS ARISING FROM THE BASE AND LACKING A SINGLE TRUNK.

9. A PLANT CONSIDERED UNDESIRABLE OR TROUBLESOME, ESPECIALLY ONE GROWING WHERE IT IS NOT WANTED, AS IN A GARDEN.

12. A TREE, SHRUB, OR PLANT HAVING FOLIAGE THAT PERSISTS AND REMAINS GREEN THROUGHOUT THE YEAR.

13. ONE OF POSSIBLY MANY CLOSELY RELATED PLANT SPECIES.

16. THE EXPANDED PART OF A LEAF OR PETAL.

17. A CHEMICAL USED TO KILL OR REPEL INSECTS.

19. THE YELLOW DUST PRODUCED BY THE ANTERS OF A PLANT. THE MALE ELEMENT THAT FERTILIZES THE OVULE.

20. BELONGING TO NEITHER KIND; NOT ONE THING OR THE OTHER. NEITHER ACID NOR ALKALINE: pH6.5-7.5.

Down

1. A PLANT GROWN FOR FLAVORING OR MEDICINAL PURPOSES.

3. THE BEGINNING OF GROWTH, AS OF A SEED, SPORE, OR BUD.

4. THE CHANGES THAT OCCUR AS PLANTS GROW, DIE, AND BREAK DOWN IN THE SOIL.

7. THE ACT OF OR THE ACTUAL SUBSTANCE ADDED TO SOIL TO PROVIDE ADDITIONAL NUTRIENTS FOR PLANTS.

8. THE GENERAL TERM USED FOR A TYPE OF GARDENING USING NO CHEMICAL OR SYNTHETIC FERTILIZERS OR PESTICIDES.

10. A PLANT WHICH GROWS IN THE SOIL.

11. THE LOOSENING OF SOIL BY DIGGING TO ALLOW AIR TO PASS FREELY.

14. A POD, SUCH AS THAT OF A PEA OR BEAN, THAT SPLITS INTO TWO VALVES WITH THE SEEDS ATTACHED TO ONE EDGE OF THE VALVES. SUCH AS SOYBEANS.

15. A MIXTURE OF DECAYING ORGANIC MATTER, AS FROM LEAVES AND MANURE, USED TO IMPROVE SOIL STRUCTURE AND PROVIDE NUTRIENTS. A COMPOSITION; A MIXTURE.

18. A PROTECTIVE COVERING PLACED AROUND PLANTS TO PREVENT THE EVAPORATION OF MOISTURE, THE FREEZING OF ROOTS, AND THE GROWTH OF WEEDS.

CROSSWORD PUZZLE 3: ANSWERS FOUND ON PAGE 37

"GROWTH IS ESSENTIAL IN THE WORD OF GOD"
SEEK AND FIND YOUR WAY THROUGH THE MAZE BELOW

START

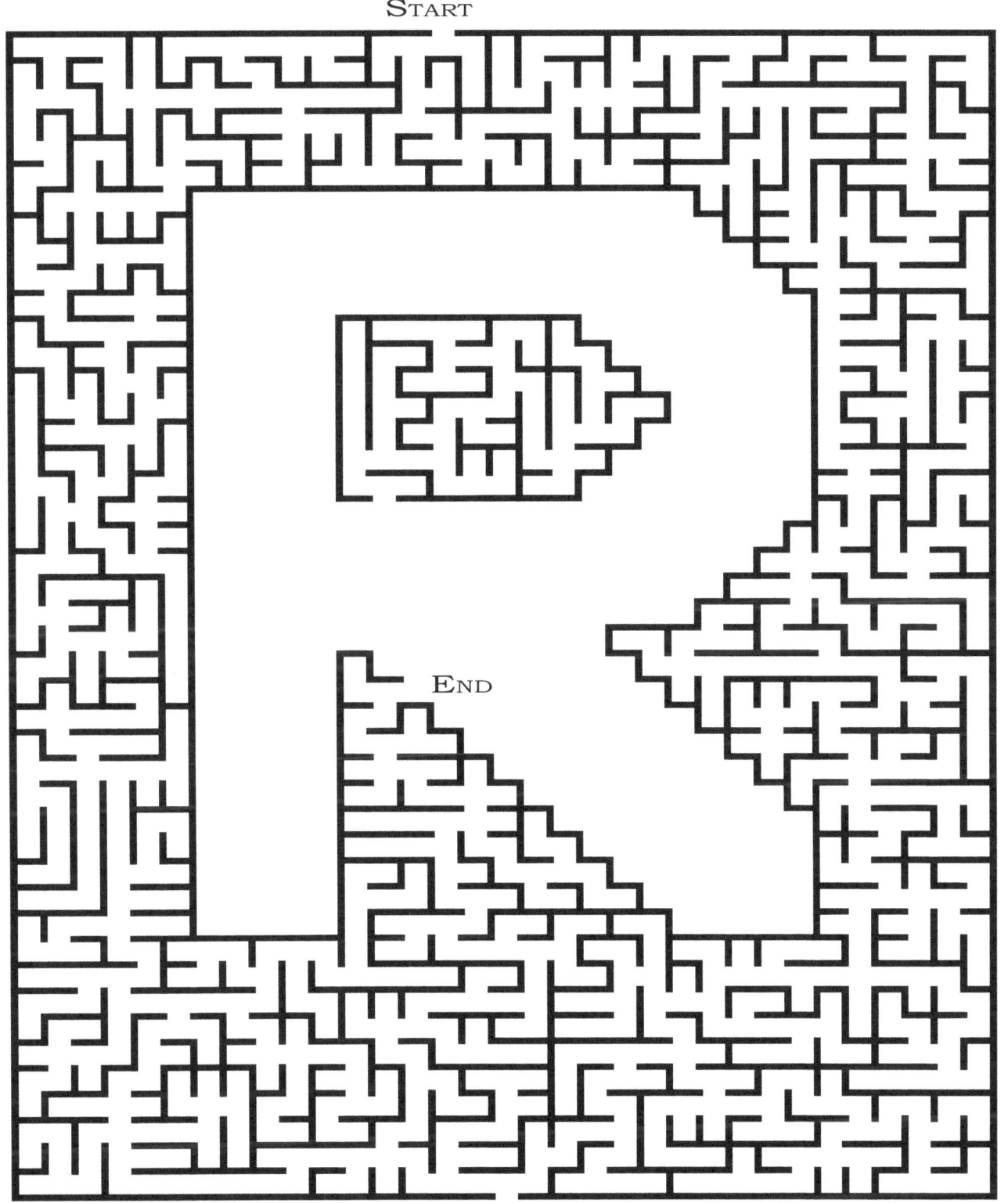

END

19

TOOLS FOR A HEALTHY GARDEN
CROSSWORD PUZZLE 4

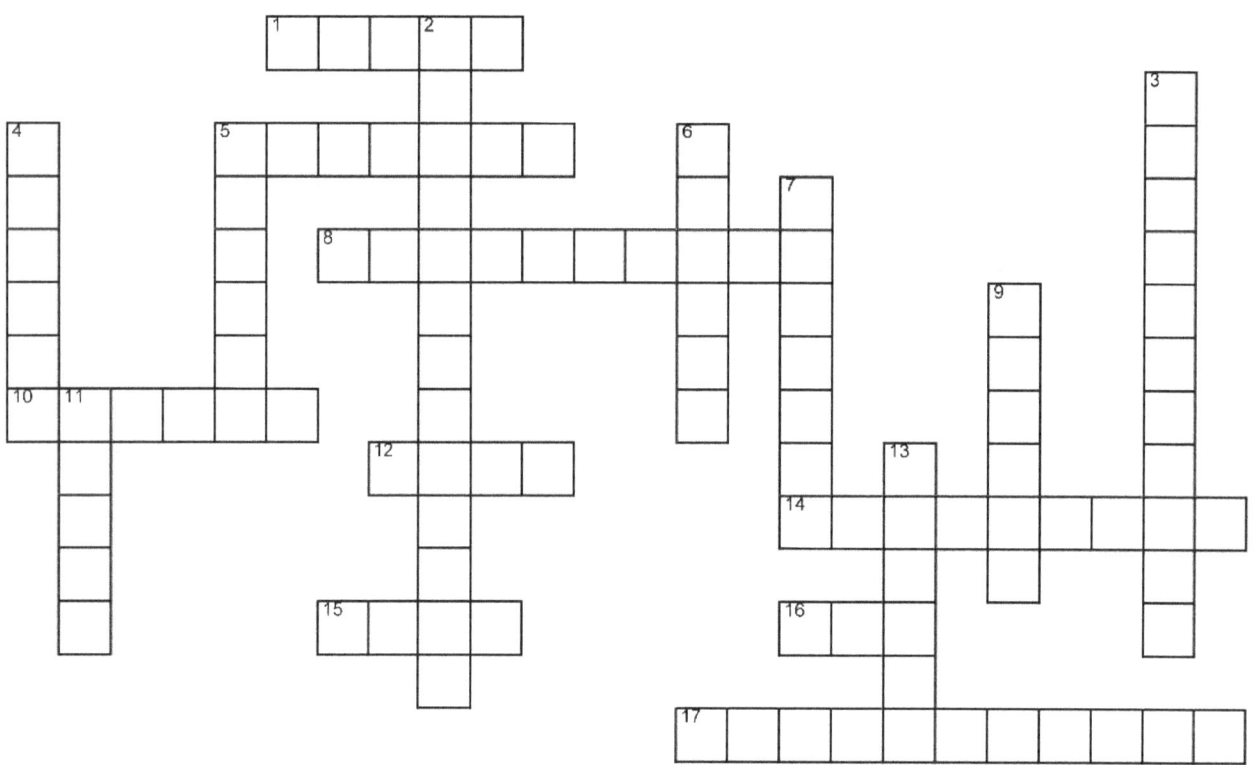

ACROSS

1. AN INSTRUMENT FOR DIGGING, CONSISTING OF A BROAD PALM WITH A HANDLE.

5. A FARM VEHICLE FOR THE PURPOSES OF HAULING A TRAILER OR MACHINERY USED IN AGRICULTURE OR CONSTRUCTION.

8. A HOLLOW TUBE DESIGNED TO CARRY FLUIDS FROM ONE LOCATION TO ANOTHER.

10. AN INSTRUMENT CONSISTING OF TWO BLADES WITH A BEVEL EDGE, MOVABLE ON A PIN, USED FOR CLIPPING OR CUTTING SMALL BRANCHES AND LEAVES.

12. AN INSTRUMENT USED FOR COLLECTING HAY OR OTHER LIGHT THINGS WHICH ARE SPREAD OVER A LARGE SURFACE.

14. IT IS A PLATE OF IRON, WITH AN EYE FOR A HANDLE, WHICH IS SET AT AN ACUTE ANGLE WITH THE PLATE.

15. AN INSTRUMENT DRAWN BY OXEN OR HORSES AND SAVES THE LABOR OF DIGGING.

16. A TOOL THAT USES A HARD BLADE OR WIRE WITH AN ABRASIVE EDGE TO CUT THROUGH SOFTER MATERIALS.

17. A SMALL HAND-PROPELLED VEHICLE, DESIGNED TO BE PUSHED AND GUIDED BY A SINGLE PERSON USING TWO HANDLES TO THE REAR.

DOWN

2. FIRM RESOLUTION; SETTLED PURPOSE; ABSOLUTE DIRECTION TO A CERTAIN END.

3. A GARDENING TOOL, WITH A HANDLE AND SEVERAL (USUALLY FOUR) SHORT, STURDY TINES. IT IS USED FOR LOOSENING, LIFTING AND TURNING OVER SOIL IN GARDENING AND FARMING.

4. A COVER FOR THE HAND, OR FOR THE HAND AND ARM, WITH A SEPARATE SHEATH FOR EACH FINGER.

5. FARM INSTRUMENT USED TO PREPARE THE GROUND FOR A CROP, AND TO KEEP IT FREE FROM WEEDS. HARROWING.

6. INSTRUMENT USED POR THROWING EARTH OR OTHER LOOSE SUBSTANCES.

7. INCLOSING WITH A FENCE; GUARDING; FORTIFYING.

9. AN INSTRUMENT DESIGNED TO EASE THE TASK OF REMOVING WEEDS FROM GARDENS AND LAWNS.

11. IN MAN, THE EXTREMITY OF THE ARM, CONSISTING OF THE PALM AND FINGERS, CONNECTED WITH THE ARM AT THE WRIST; THE PART WITH WHICH WE HOLD AND USE ANY INSTRUMENT.

13. A GARDENER'S TOOL, MADE OF IRON AND SCOOPED; USED IN TAKING UP PLANTS AND FOR OTHER PURPOSES.

CROSSWORD PUZZLE 4: ANSWERS FOUND ON PAGE 37

SECRET MESSAGE 3

A	B	C	D	E	F	G	H	I	J	K	L	M	N	O	P	Q	R	S	T	U	V	W	X	Y	Z
12	22	4	17	3	14	24	16	5	18	1	11	2	21	6	10	20	7	26	13	25	8	15	23	9	19

USE THE ABOVE KEYS TO DECODE THE MESSAGE BELOW

I (5)   WENT (15 3 21 13)   DOWN (17 6 15 21)

INTO (5 21 13 6)   THE (13 16 3)   GARDEN (24 12 7 17 3 21)

OF (6 14)   NUTS (21 25 13 26)   TO (13 6)   SEE (26 3 3)

THE (13 16 3)   FRUITS (14 7 25 5 13 26)   OF (6 14)

THE (13 16 3)   VALLEY (8 12 11 11 3 9) ,   AND (12 21 17)

TO (13 6)   SEE (26 3 3)   WHETHER (15 16 3 13 16 3 7)

THE (13 16 3)   VINE (8 5 21 3)

FLOURISHED (14 11 6 25 7 5 26 16 3 17) ,   AND (12 21 17)

THE (13 16 3)   POMEGRANATES (10 6 2 3 24 7 12 21 12 13 3 26)

BUDDED (22 25 17 17 3 17) .

WHERE IS THIS TEXT FOUND: _____

SECRET MESSAGE 3: ANSWERS FOUND ON PAGE 35

SEE HOW MANY WORDS
YOU CAN GROW OUT OF
AGRICULTURE

"WHEN JESUS HAD SPOKEN THESE WORDS, HE WENT FORTH WITH HIS DISCIPLES OVER
THE BROOK CEDRON, WHERE WAS A GARDEN, INTO THE WHICH HE ENTERED,
AND HIS DISCIPLES." ~ JOHN 18:1

GARDENING ABC's

FIND THESE WORDS IN THE FOREST OF LETTERS

```
C Q Z C Z X G H P O L L E N E K R D R L Z Z I M F
I D Y X E B E B M U X P C G Z X Q E A H U C L G E
V A F D H A R W O L I W E E D N L I C M R B K D Y
D V A N Q R M Q R S X Y G Z O C R L B B D E I S X
B L T X E D I Q Q C V B D I Y T U A U R Y C K D T
B U M M B M N G W J F D T C S M W R I N I I B G Z
K N J K E V A Y E W Z A Y E C F H I S T X A G F K
D X I R N A T H H N R A R I D S T F C K A Z L X U
Y V E V O Z I Y W E C R N P Q E V E R G R E E N G
X Q S R A G O T A E E A V M A H S L R R Q U O S S
X Y I K O R N S D T G F C H A N Z C P J J P T Q Q
P E E Z F P I A P R F I C Q I K D J L P N D E H Q
Z Q Q J N I H E O F Z N B T S A T V Z F X P Y S W
R O S E T T E Y T D W Q R Y J C R M C O M P O S T
Q T V J V K Q Z T Y V N E U T R A L Q L E G U M E
O F E R T I L I Z E R I C Z S H E R B S A A W N R
W I T U W W P I K M Y B K A O V T C Z X B M X U T
```

AERATION	BLADE	COMPOST	DECAY CYCLE
EVERGREEN	FERTILIZER	GERMINATION	HERBS
INSECTICIDE	LEGUME	MULCH	NEUTRAL
ORGANIC	POLLEN	ROSETTE	SHRUB
TERRESTRIAL	VARIETY	WEED	XEROPHYTE

23

WORD SEARCH 3: ANSWERS FOUND ON PAGE 36

FILL IN THE BLANK
COMMIT THESE VERSES OF SCRIPTURE TO MEMORY

OR IF HE SHALL ASK AN _____, WILL HE _____ HIM A _____? ~ LUKE 11:12

AND THE RAIN _____, AND THE _____ CAME, AND THE _____ BLEW, AND _____ UPON THAT _____; AND IT _____: AND _____ WAS THE _____ OF IT. ~ MATTHEW 7:27

THEN SAID THE _____ TO THE _____, BIND HIM _____ AND _____, AND _____ HIM AWAY, AND _____ HIM INTO OUTER _____; THERE SHALL BE _____ AND _____ OF _____. ~ MATTHEW 22:13

NEITHER DO MEN _____ A _____, AND PUT IT _____ A _____, BUT ON A _____; AND IT _____ LIGHT UNTO ALL THAT ARE IN THE _____.
~ MATTHEW 5:15

NEITHER DO _____ PUT NEW _____ INTO OLD _____: ELSE THE _____ _____, AND THE WINE _____ OUT, AND THE BOTTLES _____: BUT THEY PUT _____ WINE INTO _____ BOTTLES, AND _____ ARE _____.
~ MATTHEW 9:17

AND HE _____ A _____ UNTO THEM, CAN THE _____ LEAD THE BLIND? SHALL _____ NOT BOTH _____ INTO THE _____? ~ LUKE 6:39

HOW _____ YE? IF A _____ HAVE AN HUNDRED _____, AND _____ OF THEM BE GONE _____, DOTH HE NOT _____ THE _____ AND _____, AND _____ INTO THE _____, AND _____ THAT WHICH IS GONE _____?
~ MATTHEW 18:12

BUT _____ THAT HAD _____ ONE WENT AND _____ IN THE _____, AND _____ HIS LORD'S _____. ~ MATTHEW 25:18

UNSCRAMBLE THESE WORDS THAT PROMOTE GROWTH

STOPMCO   _____

CRINGOA   _____

ROHWAWERBLE   _____

DPSEA   _____

LWOP   _____

OLTWRE   _____

ENIDMAOEINTRT   _____

UNSCRAMBLE EXERCISE 2: ANSWERS FOUND ON PAGE 34

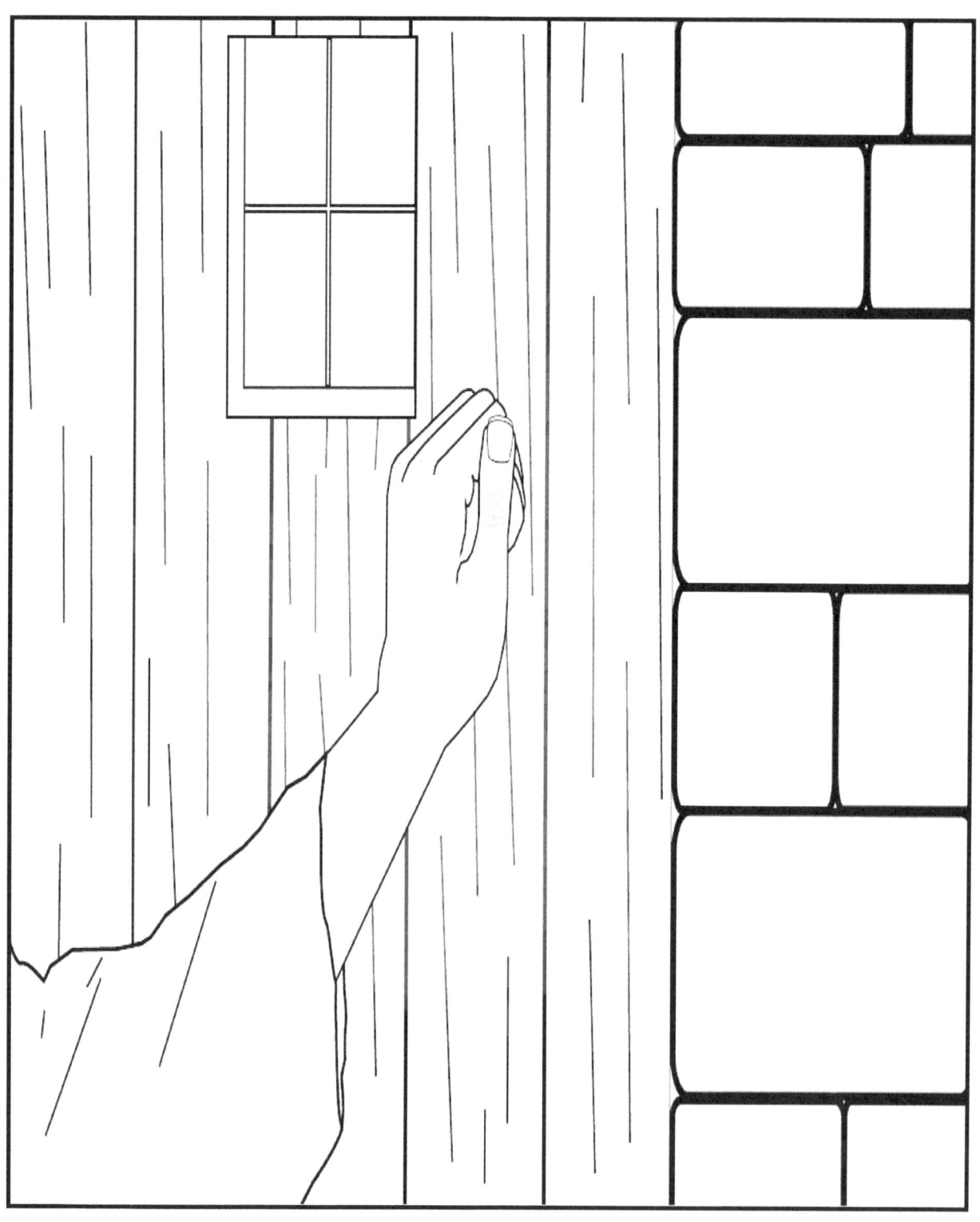

THE KNOCK

"GROWTH IS ESSENTIAL IN THE WORD OF GOD"

SEEK AND FIND YOUR WAY THROUGH THE MAZE BELOW

END

START

SEE HOW MANY WORDS
YOU CAN GROW OUT OF
COMPOST

"IT WAS PLANTED IN A GOOD SOIL BY GREAT WATERS, THAT IT MIGHT BRING FORTH BRANCHES, AND THAT IT MIGHT BEAR FRUIT, THAT IT MIGHT BE A GOODLY VINE." ~ EZEKIEL 17:8

_____

_____

_____

_____   _____

_____   _____

_____   _____

_____   _____

SECRET MESSAGE 4

A	B	C	D	E	F	G	H	I	J	K	L	M	N	O	P	Q	R	S	T	U	V	W	X	Y	Z
24	8	16	1	15	26	10	3	17	4	13	23	14	7	18	22	6	19	12	25	11	20	2	9	21	5

USE THE ABOVE KEYS TO DECODE THE MESSAGE BELOW

24 7 1   18 11 25   18 26   25 3 15

10 19 18 11 7 1   14 24 1 15   25 3 15

23 18 19 1   10 18 1   25 18   10 19 18 2

15 20 15 19 21   25 19 15 15   25 3 24 25

17 12   22 23 15 24 12 24 7 25   25 18

25 3 15   12 17 10 3 25 ,   24 7 1

10 18 18 1   26 18 19   26 18 18 1 ;

25 3 15   25 19 15 15   18 26   23 17 26 15

24 23 12 18   17 7   25 3 15   14 17 1 12 25

18 26   25 3 15   10 24 19 1 15 7 ,   24 7 1

25 3 15   25 19 15 15   18 26

13 7 18 2 23 15 1 10 15   18 26   10 18 18 1

24 7 1   15 20 17 23 .

WHERE IS THIS TEXT FOUND: _____

SECRET MESSAGE 4: ANSWERS FOUND ON PAGE 35

BIBLE TRIVIA 2: LESSONS FROM THE PARABLES

1. IN THE PARABLE OF THE MARRIAGE FEAST, WHAT HAPPENED TO THE MAN THAT WAS NOT WEARING A WEDDING ROBE?
A) THROWN INTO PRISON   B) CAST INTO DARKNESS   C) CRUCIFIED   D) EXILED

2. JESUS QUOTES A PORTION OF TEXT FROM THE OLD TESTAMENT IN ONE OF HIS PARABLES. THE STONE WHICH THE BUILDERS REJECTED IS BECOME THE HEAD OF THE CORNER. WHICH OLD TESTAMENT BOOK DID THIS COME FROM?
A) PSALM   B) ISAIAH   C) EZEKIEL   D) JEREMIAH

3. WHERE DID THE MAN WHO RECEIVED ONE TALENT HIDE IT?
A) IN A POT   B) IN A CAVE   C) IN THE GROUND   D) IN THE FIREPLACE

4. IN THE PARABLE OF THE CLOTH AND WINE, WHY DIDN'T ANY MAN PUT NEW WINE INTO OLD BOTTLES?
A) IT WILL BURST THE BOTTLES   B) IT WILL TASTE BAD   C) IT WILL SMELL BAD   D) THE WINE WILL NOT AGE

5. THE HOUSE BUILT ON SAND WAS KNOCKED DOWN BY WHAT?
A) RIVER   B) TORNADO   C) HURRICANE   D) FLOOD

6. JESUS ASKED: 'CAN THE BLIND LEAD THE....?'
A) LAME   B) SIGHTED   C) DEAF   D) BLIND

7. IN THE PARABLE OF THE LAMP, WHERE DO YOU SET IT ONCE IT IS LIT?
A) ON A CANDLESTICK   B) IN THE HALLWAY   C) UNDER A BUSHEL   D) IN THE WINDOW

8. IN THE PARABLE OF THE GOOD FATHER, IF A SON ASKS FOR AN EGG, WHAT WOULD THE GOOD FATHER NOT GIVE HIM?
A) A FISH   B) A STONE   C) A SCORPION   D) A MOUSE

9. IN THE PARABLE OF THE LEAVEN, WHAT IS LEAVEN MORE COMMONLY KNOWN AS?
A) FLOUR   B) YEAST   C) BREAD   D) SALT

10. WHAT DOES THE SHEPHERD OF THE SHEEP DO ONCE HE REALIZES ONE IS MISSING?
A) WAITS UP ALL NIGHT LOOKS FOR IT TO RETURN   B) ABANDONS IT AND GOES HOME   C) REPORTS IT TO HIS MASTER   D) GOES AND LOOKS FOR IT

BIBLE TRIVIA 2: ANSWERS FOUND ON PAGE 34

GARDENING TOOLS
FIND THESE WORDS IN THE FOREST OF LETTERS

```
P J D V X S P H R T N R A S Y Z R J E B F Q V R U
A L S Z S Z Y Y W Z F E N C I N G R V Y J E U U Q
N W N V X M A A E X X Q S F C R S H O V E L X G E
I Z K W X R S I Z F T W H W V Q X T A A Z V A N X
T P F H F Q H J I T R E E I R G K H K K A I O D F
O Q D E L F A H B R A L A K N F A R W F A I D L Y
X K O E X I R N O C S R O Q V O R F M T V P F Q
I G R L J W D R G W T G S W I F Y Y D A H H F J C
S E R B C E S G C E O Y J H G J D T N E L F D O E
H M I A J E Z L F L R H P N M X O I G Q N E P O H
I V H R K D Z O Y S S J I Z E Q M L G S C H H V E
V M P R A E M V Q T T D M H B R W L G K X N O V E
T Y L O O R I E F O A I I C E V C E R Q E F O S E
P J O W U P D S Q P T J D T V Y F R L D T P N O E
N J W X M F U U S P A D E R A E R E R W R S X A X
O F R B Y E H J B G C D C H N U A Y P J R X W Q
Q T W X X K T X O E W J U M U H G U A J R A K E N
```

FENCING	DETERMINATION	SPADE
PLOW	RAKE	SHOVEL
GARDEN HOE	TROWEL	TRACTOR
TILLER	WHEEL BARROW	GARDEN HOSE
SHEARS	SPADING FORK	WEEDER
SAW	GLOVES	HANDS

WORD SEARCH 4: ANSWERS FOUND ON PAGE 36

SEE HOW MANY WORDS
YOU CAN GROW OUT OF
VINEYARD

"AND AT THE SEASON HE SENT TO THE HUSBANDMEN A SERVANT, THAT HE MIGHT RECEIVE FROM THE HUSBANDMEN OF THE FRUIT OF THE VINEYARD." ~ MARK 12:2

"GROWTH IS ESSENTIAL IN THE WORD OF GOD"
SEEK AND FIND YOUR WAY THROUGH THE MAZE BELOW

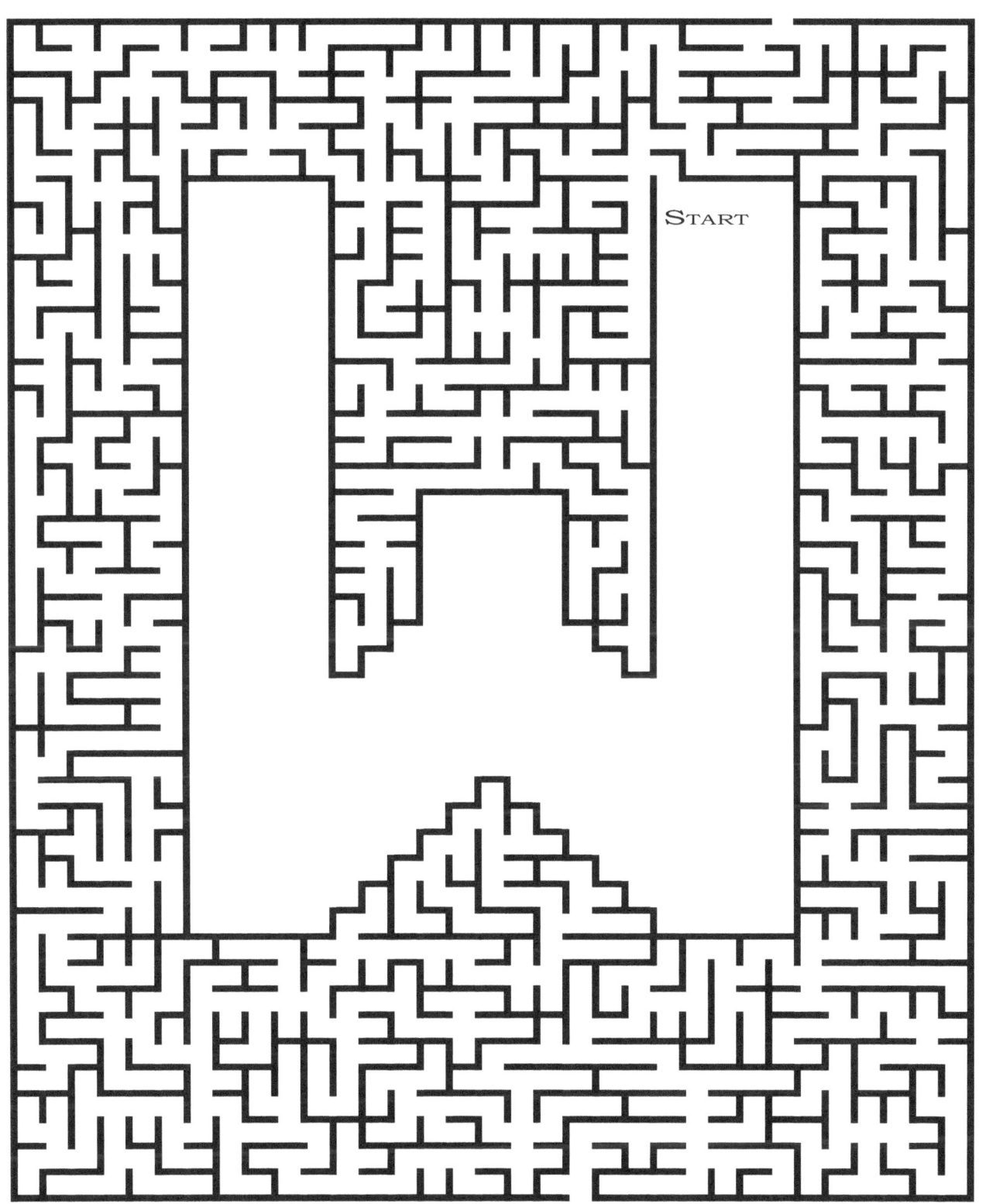

START

END

ANSWER PAGES

UNSCRAMBLE EXERCISE 1

EHRTVSA	HARVEST
INSWETS	WITNESS
CFIPNROTEE	PERFECTION
VEIESCR	SERVICE
WOMDIS	WISDOM
EGRCA	GRACE
FACTNOTSICANII	SANCTIFICATION
PNIAIPLTCOA	APPLICATION
SAILTR	TRIALS
HYCITRA	CHARITY

BIBLE TRIVIA 1

1. A
2. B
3. A
4. D
5. A
6. B
7. C
8. D
9. A
10. B

UNSCRAMBLE EXERCISE 2

STOPMCO	COMPOST
CRINGOA	ORGANIC
ROHWAWERBLE	WHEELBARROW
DPSEA	SPADE
LWOP	PLOW
OLTWRE	TROWEL
ENIDMAOEINTRT	DETERMINATION

BIBLE TRIVIA 2

1. B
2. A
3. C
4. A
5. D
6. D
7. A
8. C
9. B
10. D

SECRET MESSAGE 1

THOU SHALT NOT SOW THY VINEYARD
WITH DIVERS SEEDS: LEST THE FRUIT
OF THY SEED WHICH THOU HAST SOWN,
AND THE FRUIT OF THY VINEYARD, BE
DEFILED.

DEUTERONOMY 22:9

SECRET MESSAGE 2

AND SOW THE FIELDS, AND PLANT VINE-
YARDS, WHICH MAY YIELD FRUITS OF
INCREASE.

PSALM 107:37

SECRET MESSAGE 3

I WENT DOWN INTO THE GARDEN OF NUTS
TO SEE THE FRUITS OF THE VALLEY, AND TO SEE
WHETHER THE VINE FLOURISHED,
AND THE POMEGRANATES BUDDED.

SONG OF SOLOMON 6:11

SECRET MESSAGE 4

AND OUT OF THE GROUND MADE THE
LORD GOD TO GROW EVERY TREE THAT IS
PLEASANT TO THE SIGHT, AND GOOD FOR
FOOD; THE TREE OF LIFE ALSO IN THE
MIDST OF THE GARDEN, AND THE TREE OF
KNOWLEDGE OF GOOD AND EVIL.

GENESIS 2:9

SECRET PHRASE 1

SEED SOWING

SECRET PHRASE 2

HARVESTING TIME

WORD SEARCH 1

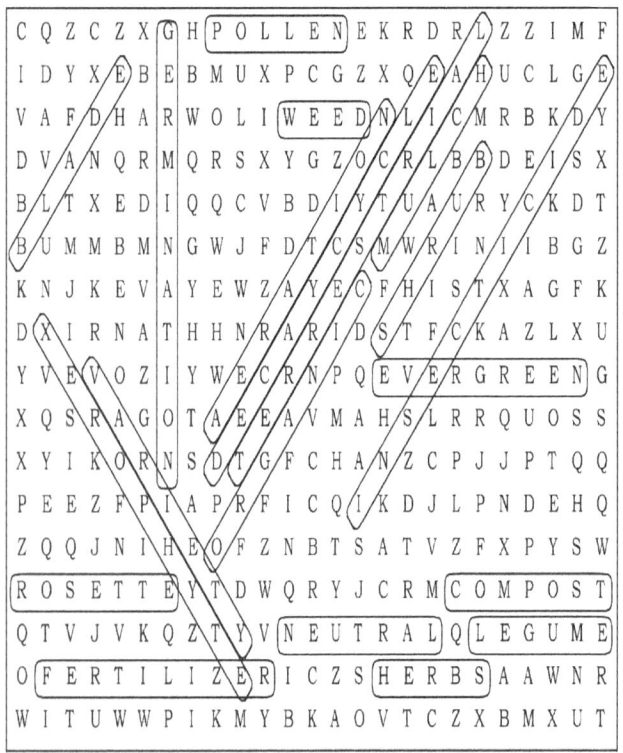

```
R K I L V T G X P R A Y E R S O W Y U S Z U T A A
P K S L B G R B L K V W I T N E S S N U F N H W A
S P K E I V O E J N F B F Y F N W D C U B E W A
P E S I R W W C A A H M F Q B O T N E M N Y K Q Z
I G O K J V N I R L W Y T Z I J J I R O J W U Y K
P U A Z D E I A A Y S F Q T A P D Q S D Y G M Z O
L M Y T I P H C T K W F A V R E Q G T N S O G Q N
C O K D H C E I E J Y C S K E V C G A C E S P L W
U U E L A N L R S D I Y T S A S D N N B L P X O J
U B P E K I T G F L F C U G P T M P D S F E M B D
O L T X M K C I P E A B D T I D M O I P D L A E A
H J D U R V S P K D C X Y S N W W L N M E F W B Z
R D H H V D A N A W J T A B G D P G X N M V D
Y L H A R V E S T V D I J I H I J I A E N I R I E Q
Q I U E D T E M P T A T I O N F I U I C A G R R L
Z K R F D V Y S B V G W K A N P O M G L C S H X
Y S I C K L E W M E E K N E S S G D V M U K V T J
```

WORD SEARCH 2

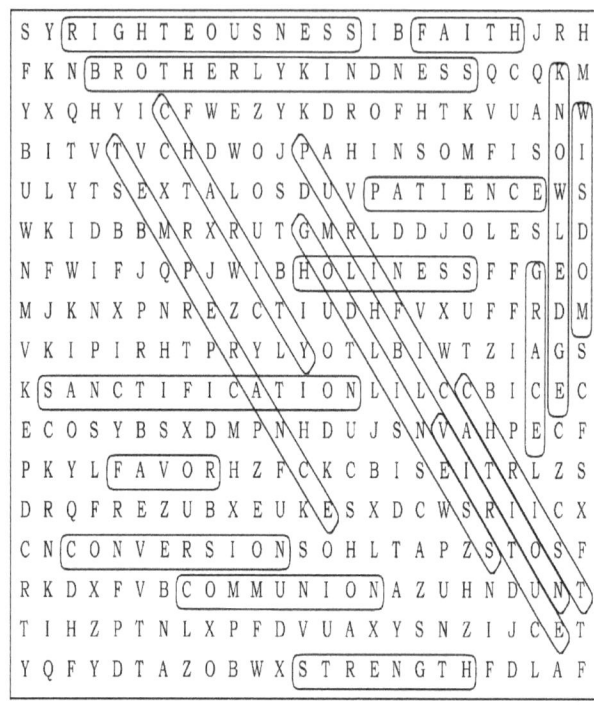

```
S Y R I G H T E O U S N E S S I B F A I T H J R H
F K N B R O T H E R L Y K I N D N E S S Q C Q K M
Y X Q H Y I C F W E Z Y K D R O F H T K V U A N W
B I T V T V C H D W O J P A H I N S O M F I S O I
U L Y T S E X T A L O S D U V P A T I E N C E W S
W K I D B B M R X R U T G M R L D D J O L E S L D
N F W I F J Q P J W I B H O L I N E S S F F G E O
M J K N X P N R E Z C T I U D H F V X U F F R D M
V K I P I R H T P R Y L Y O T L B I W T Z I A G S
K S A N C T I F I C A T I O N L I L C C B I C E C
E C O S Y B S X D M P N H D U J S N V A H P E C F
P K Y L F A V O R H Z F C K C B I S E I T R L Z S
D R Q F R E Z U B X E U K E S X D C W S R I I C X
C N C O N V E R S I O N S O H L T A P Z S T O S F
R K D X F V B C O M M U N I O N A Z U H N D U N T
T I H Z P T N L X P F D V U A X Y S N Z I J C E T
Y Q F Y D T A Z O B W X S T R E N G T H F D L A F
```

WORD SEARCH 3

```
C Q Z C Z X G H P O L L E N E K R D R L Z Z I M F
I D Y X E B E B M U X P C G Z X Q E A H U C L G E
V A F D H A R W O L I W E E D N L I C M R B K D Y
D V A N Q R M Q R S X Y G Z O C R L B B D E I S X
B L T X E D I Q Q C V B D I Y T U A U R Y C K D T
B U M M B M N G W J F D T C S M W R I N I I B G Z
K N J K E V A Y E W Z A Y E C F H I S T X A G F K
D X I R N A T H H N R A R I D S T F C K A Z L X U
Y V E V O Z I Y W E C R N P Q E V E R G R E E N G
X Q S R A G O T A E E A V M A H S L R R Q U O S S
X Y I K O R N S D T G F C H A N Z C P J J P T Q Q
P E E Z F P I A P R F I C Q I K D J L P N D E H Q
Z Q Q J N I H E O F Z N B T S A T V Z F X P Y S W
R O S E T T E Y T D W Q R Y J C R M C O M P O S T
Q T V J V K Q Z T Y N E U T R A L Q L E G U M E
O F E R T I L I Z E R I C Z S H E R B S A A W N R
W I T U W W P I K M Y B K A O V T C Z X B M X U T
```

WORD SEARCH 4

```
P J D V X S P H R T N R A S Y Z R J E B F Q V R U
A L S Z S Z Y Y W Z F E N C I N G R V Y J E U U Q
N W N V X M A E X X Q S F C R S H O V E L X G E
I Z K W X R S I Z F T W H V Q X T A A Z V A N X
T P F H F Q H J I T R E E I R G K H K K A I O D F
O Q D E L F A H B R A L A K N F A R W F A I D L Y
X K O E X I N R N O C S R O Q V O R F M T V P F Q
I G R L J W D R G W T G S W I F Y Y D A H H F J C
S E R B C E S G C E O Y J H G J D T N E L F D O E
H M I A J E Z L F L R H P N M X O I G Q N E P O H
I V H R K D Z O Y S S J Z E Q M L G S C H H V E
V M P R A E M V Q T T D M H B R W L G K X N O V E
T Y L O O R I E F O A I I C E V C E R Q E F O S E
P J O W U P D S Q P T J D T V Y F R L D T P N O E
N J W X M F U U S P A D E R A E R E R W R S X A X
O F R B Y E H J B G C D N C H N U A Y P J R X W Q
Q T W X X K T X O E W J U M U H G U A J R A K E N
```

CROSSWORD 1

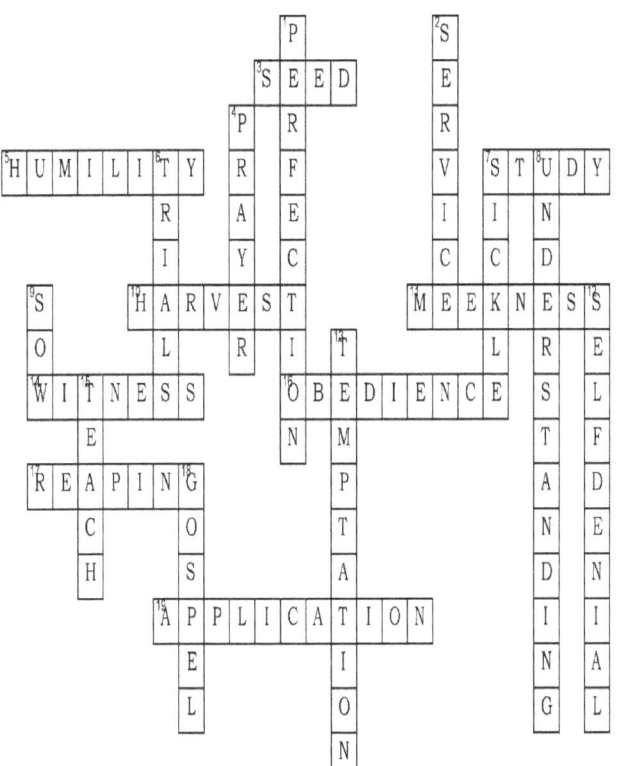

CROSSWORD 2

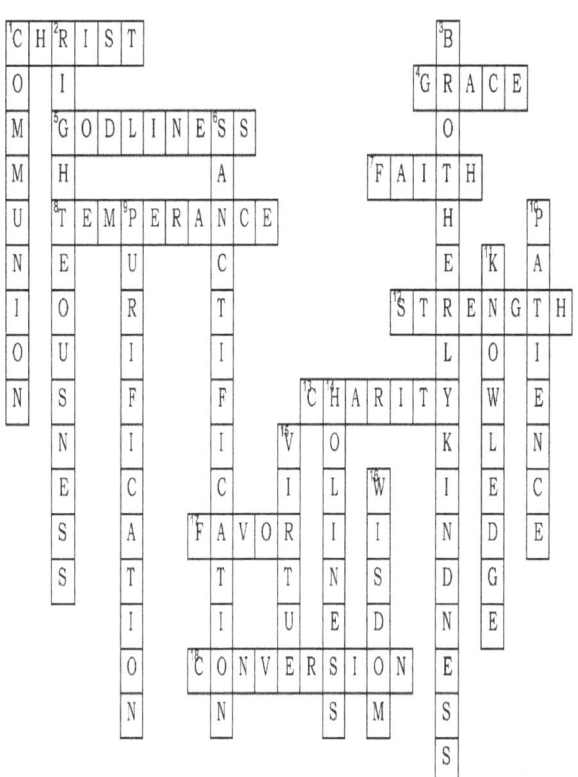

CROSSWORD 3

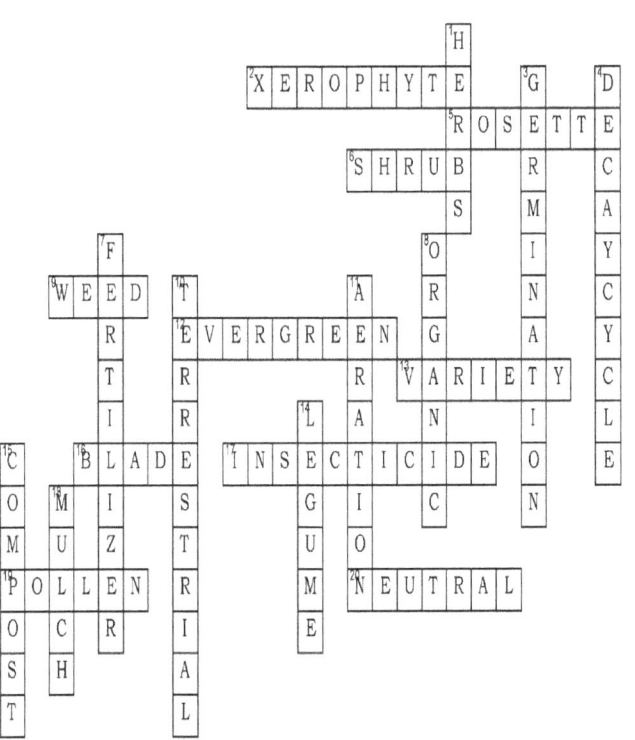

CROSSWORD 4

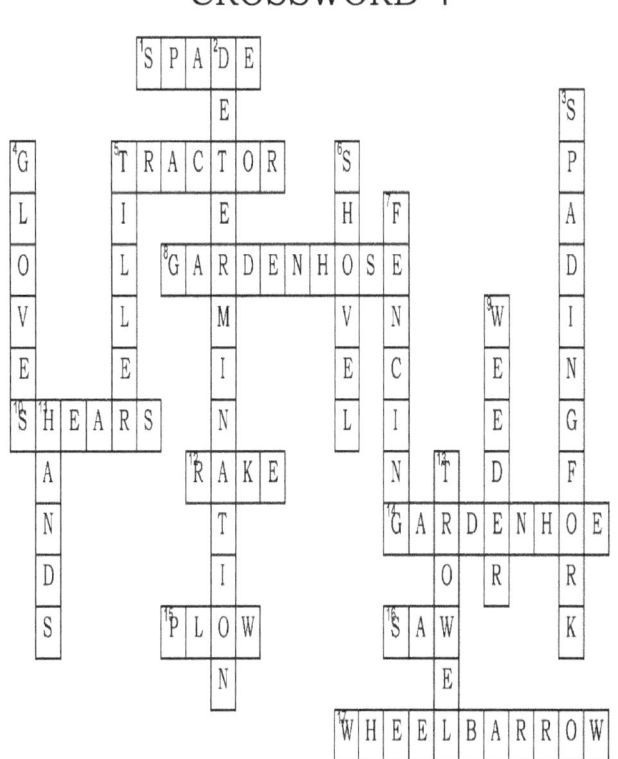

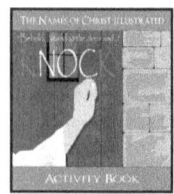

THE NOC ILLUSTRATED
ACTIVITY BOOK

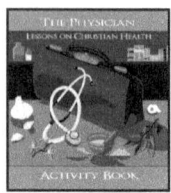

THE PHYSICIAN:
CHRISTIAN HEALTH

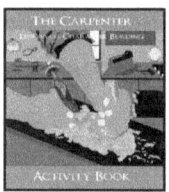

THE CARPENTER:
CHARACTER BUILDING

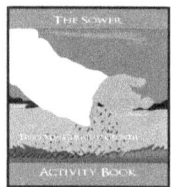

THE SOWER:
CHRISTIAN GROWTH

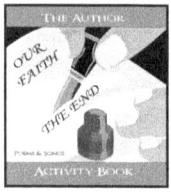

THE AUTHOR:
POEMS & SONGS

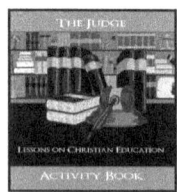

THE JUDGE:
CHRISTIAN EDUCATION

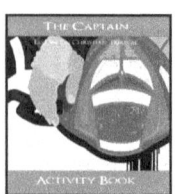

THE CAPTAIN:
CHRISTIAN PURPOSE

"PORTRAITS OF THE SAVIOUR'S
DESIRE TO ENTER HEARTS."

THIS BOOK:

THE SOWER

LESSONS ON CHRISTIAN GROWTH

THE NAMES OF CHRIST ILLUSTRATED

PLEASE VISIT US ONLINE TO VIEW
MORE GREAT TITLES AT:

WWW.THENOCILLUSTRATED.COM

www.ingramcontent.com/pod-product-compliance
Lightning Source LLC
Chambersburg PA
CBHW081239170526
45165CB00009B/3117